MIND
MAGIC

MIND MAGIC

TRICKS FOR READING MINDS

BY ORMOND McGILL

**DRAWINGS BY
ANNE CANEVARI GREEN**

THE MILLBROOK PRESS • BROOKFIELD, CONNECTICUT

Library of Congress Cataloging-in-Publication Data
McGill, Ormond.
Mind magic : tricks for reading minds / by Ormond McGill ;
drawings by Anne Canevari Green.
p.   cm.
Includes index.
Summary: Step-by-step instructions for tricks with paper
and cards that make you appear to read people's minds.
ISBN 1-56294-465-7 (lib. bdg.)
1. Tricks—Juvenile literature.   2. Card tricks—Juvenile
literature.   3. Telepathy—Juvenile literature.   [1. Magic tricks.
2. Card tricks.]   I. Green, Anne Canevari, ill.   II. Title.
GV1548.M25 1995 793.8'7—dc20 94-20324 CIP AC

Published by The Millbrook Press, Inc.
2 Old New Milford Road, Brookfield, Connecticut 06804

CONTENTS

MIND
MAGIC

A WORD FROM
THE MAGICIAN

When you perform the following tricks, you will seem to possess magical powers. Your friends will think that you can read their minds, see objects that are hidden from sight, and predict the future. In short, you will become a mastermind!

Mind magic is very entertaining because everyone is fascinated by the possibility of the magical things the mind can do. Magicians—or mentalists—such as Joseph Dunninger, George Joseph Kresge, Jr. (Kreskin), David Roy, Max Maven, and many others have specialized in this sort of magic. Now you can join them.

Keep the secrets to yourself, though. Your spectators will swamp you with questions about how you did these tricks. Don't tell them. Keep them guessing. All the fun is in the mystery. When someone asks you to tell them your secrets, tap your forehead and say, "The secrets are all up here."

When you do mind magic, perform a little seriously. Think ahead about how to best present your tricks. You are a performer, and your audience will respond to your attitude as much as to the tricks themselves. Do not claim supernatural powers for yourself. Remember, you are an entertainer, not a mystic. And now for the show!

ORMOND MCGILL

NAME THE NAME

To perform this trick, you will need nine blank business cards (which you can get from any printer). Or you can cut your own cards—about 2 by 3½ inches (5 by 9 centimeters)—out of stiff paper. In bold letters, write one of the following names on each card:

ALICE	DAISY	MOLLY
HARRY	JAMES	HENRY
PERCY	JAMES	AGNES

HERE'S WHAT YOU APPEAR TO DO

Start the trick by calling attention to the fact that each card has a different name. Ask a spectator to mix the cards and to think of one of the names. Then take back the cards and deal them out twice, faceup. As you regather the cards, say the name that the spectator is thinking of. Now climax the mystery by spelling out that name as you deal one card at a time on the table facedown, letter by letter. On turning over the card that you were holding when you spelled the last letter of the name, it proves to be the card with the selected name.

HERE'S HOW IT WORKS

Show your audience the nine name cards. Then have the cards shuffled and ask a spectator to think of one of the names. Take the cards back. Deal the first three cards faceup in one pile, the next three in a second pile, and the last three in a third pile. Now ask the spectator to show you the pile where her name card lies. Place this pile between the other two when you pick them up.

Next, deal the cards out faceup. This time, start a new pile with each of the first three cards. Continue dealing by placing the fourth card on top of the first card (pile number one), the fifth card on top of the second card (pile number two), and the sixth card on top of the third card (pile number three). The seventh card goes on pile one, the eighth on pile two, and the ninth on pile three.

Ask the spectator again to tell which pile the chosen card is in. When she does this, pick up this pile and, with the names of the cards facing you, note the middle card of the pile. This reveals the name she has selected in her mind. Remember this name and place the pile between the other two as you did before. Turn over the entire stack of cards so that they are facedown.

Now tell the spectator to concentrate on the name she thought of, and you will read her mind. Dramatically call out the name that you remember from the middle pile, and you will be correct.

Note the subtle psychology of your handling of mind magic. Do not tell your spectator to think of the name on the card; just tell her to think of the name. The audience forgets about the cards, and when you call out the very name that she is thinking of, it seems as though you have read her mind.

While you are revealing the name, you have been holding the stack of cards facedown. For the finale, deal the cards out facedown from the top of the stack, one card for each letter of the chosen name. When you reach the last letter, turn the card over. The name will stare them in the face!

Your audience is almost certain to ask you to repeat the trick. Don't do it. Do another trick instead.

NAME THE STATE

This is a good trick to perform when your audience asks you to repeat your mind-reading trick with names. Say that you will try it with the names of states this time.

You will need six blank business-size cards just like the ones you used to name the names. With a black felt pen write in bold letters the following states' names on these cards:

ARIZONA CALIFORNIA

ARKANSAS MISSISSIPPI

WISCONSIN WEST VIRGINIA

Get out your watercolors and paint the back of the ARIZONA card red. Leave the back of the ARKANSAS card alone. This will be your white card. Paint the back of the WISCONSIN card blue, the back of CALIFORNIA yellow, MISSISSIPPI orange, and WEST VIRGINIA green.

You are ready to perform.

HERE'S WHAT YOU
APPEAR TO DO

Lay out the state cards in any order on the table, state side up. Ask a spectator to think of one of the states. Then turn the cards facedown on the table (their colored sides will be faceup), and mix them up. Ask the spectator to concentrate on the state he secretly selected and request that he silently spell out the state's name—one letter at a time—as you tap on the back of each card. Ask him to tell you to stop tapping when you reach the last letter of the name that he is spelling.

When this last letter is reached, turn over the card and show your spectator the name of the state he was thinking of. It's mind magic!

HERE'S HOW IT WORKS

Each state used in this trick is spelled with a different number of letters in it: ARIZONA has seven letters; ARKANSAS has eight; WISCONSIN has nine; CALIFORNIA has ten; MISSISSIPPI has eleven; WEST VIRGINIA has twelve. Memorize the color sequence of these cards: red, white, blue, yellow, orange, green. It's easy.

Ask a spectator to look over the cards and then place them on the table faceup in any order. Have the spectator select any state he desires. Then turn the cards facedown and mix them up so that no one knows where any of the states are.

Now start tapping the back of each card in random order. You may tap any of the cards for the first six taps, but on the seventh tap follow the memorized color sequence. Tap the red card on seven, the white card on eight, the blue card on nine, the yellow card on ten, the orange card on eleven, and the green card on twelve. When the spectator tells you to stop, your last tap will fall automatically on the name of the state he has selected.

Turn the card over, and there it is!

TAP AND SPELL

For this trick you will need to use the five objects shown below: Place them in a row on the table, and you are ready to read your spectator's mind.

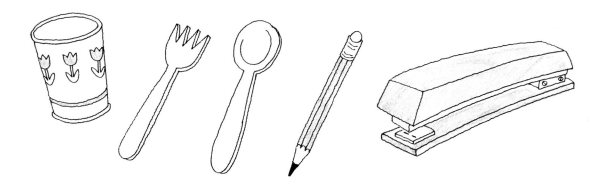

HERE'S WHAT YOU APPEAR TO DO	While your back is turned, ask a spectator to concentrate on one of these objects. Turn around and ask the spectator to turn her back. Tell her that you are going to tap the objects on the table, each in turn. Every time you tap, you want her to spell to herself—letter by letter—the name of her secretly selected object. For example, if she selected the spoon, as you tap, she would spell to herself S–P–O–O–N.
	When you tap the last letter that spells the name of her object, she is to tell you to stop. When she turns around, she will be surprised to find that with your last tap you have selected the object that she has chosen in her mind.
HERE'S HOW IT WORKS	The secret of the trick is that the names of these five objects have letters numbering from three through seven. After the spectator turns her back and you start tapping, tap any two objects at first and—just as in the Name the States trick—make your third tap on the cup, the fourth tap on the fork, the fifth tap on the spoon, the sixth on the pencil, and the seventh on the stapler. In this way, you will always finish your tapping (when the spectator tells you to stop) on her mentally selected object.

A TOTAL MYSTERY

All you will need for this trick are a pencil, a pad of paper, and an envelope. The only other requirement is a good head for numbers.

HERE'S WHAT YOU
APPEAR TO DO

Tell your spectators that you are going to predict the total of a series of numbers that they will come up with.

  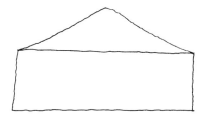

Think hard for a moment and then write a number on a slip of paper, seal it in an envelope, and give it to someone to hold.

Taking your pad and pencil, ask various people to call out any single digit number (from 1 to 10) that they wish. As the numbers are called out, jot each one on the pad in a column ready for adding. When you have made a sizable column of numbers, draw a line beneath it and ask someone to add the numbers and announce the total.

The spectator who is holding your prediction in the sealed envelope tears open the envelope and reads the total you wrote down in advance. Your prediction is 100 percent correct!

HERE'S HOW
IT WORKS

As the spectators call out numbers from 1 to 9, write them in a column on the paper. Write the first three numbers as they are called. Now comes the tricky part: After you have written down the first three numbers, leave a space for a number to be written in later, as shown in the drawing on the next page.

Proceed to write the numbers as they are called. As you write them, add them mentally until you reach a sum

6
1
3

8
5
2
4
1
5
___

AFTER WRITING THE COLUMN OF NUMBERS THE SPECTATORS CALL OUT, WRITE IN THE REQUIRED NUMBER (FROM ONE TO NINE) TO MAKE THE TOTAL MATCH YOUR PREDICTION.

slightly less than the total you have written on the slip in the sealed envelope. In the above example, the magician had written 40 as the predicted total number. She told the spectators to stop when they reached a total of 35. While pretending to add up the column, all she does is to slip in a five in the space left in the column.

When the magician shows the pad of paper to the audience, they will see the following column:

Be careful! Keep asking for numbers only until the spectators have reached a sum that is nine short of your predicted total. Suppose, for example, that your predicted total was 40. If the sum has reached 31, you can request another number and write it in the column. The most this number could be is 9, so you are safe in doing this.

One number added to a column of numbers is never noticed. Hand the pad to a spectator, who adds the numbers and calls out the total. Then have another spectator open the sealed envelope and call out the total predicted on the slip of paper. They match!

OPEN SESAME!

You will need six keys for this trick: one that opens a lock (this could be a padlock or a lock on a door, a cupboard, or a box) and five assorted keys that do not open the lock you are using in your show. You will also need a small bead and six envelopes.

HERE'S WHAT YOU APPEAR TO DO

You patter: *Ladies and gentlemen, there is a physical phenomenon known as psychometry. This is the psychic connection between objects and their owners. I have attempted to create an experiment that will show you this principle in operation. Since a key will*

always fit in its lock, I will use these objects to demonstrate psychometry to you as best I can.

I have here one lock and six keys. One and only one of the keys belongs to this particular lock; in other words, it has a psychometric association with it. Please test this fact.

A spectator tries out the six keys and finds that only one of them will open the door.

You continue to patter: *Now that you know what I have said is true, I propose this experiment in psychometry. We will seal each key in an identical envelope. The envelopes will be thoroughly mixed, so there is no possible way for me to know which envelope holds the key that opens this door.*

I will then take one envelope at a time and hold it over the lock. I will try to sense the psychometric tie between the correct key and its owner. Let us begin!

Seal the six keys in separate envelopes. A spectator mixes them and hands them back to you. One by one, hold an envelope near the lock, concentrating very hard as you do so. Finally, one "feels" right to your psychometric intuition. Tear open this envelope, and it proves to hold the only key that will open the lock.

HERE'S HOW IT WORKS

The lock and keys are quite ordinary and not prepared in any way. All may be examined, and only one of the six keys will open the lock, exactly as you have said. However, you use a secret "gimmick" that makes it possible to do the trick. This gimmick is in the form of a small bead that you have concealed in the fold of the palm of your hand as you start the trick. (This technique is known as "palming.")

Hand out the six envelopes for examination and show that only one of the keys will open the lock. Drop the key used to open the lock into an envelope. Seal the envelope and hand it to a spectator. Now the secret: As you drop the key into the envelope, you secretly drop the bead in along with it.

Each of the other keys is also placed in an envelope and sealed. A spectator mixes them thoroughly. Take back the stack of mixed envelopes and tap them down against the palm of your hand. This moves the bead to the lower corner of its envelope. By feeling the lower corners of the envelopes, you will know which envelope contains the bead.

Perform the showmanship of passing the envelopes in front of the lock in search of the psychometric link. When you have done this long enough, tear open the envelope that holds the bead (and the correct key). Do this by grasp-

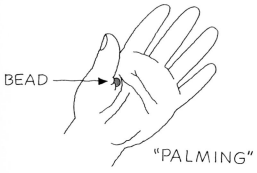

BEAD

"PALMING"

ing the envelope with your thumb and forefinger at the corner where the bead is hidden.

Tip the envelope so that the key slides to the opposite corner. You are holding the bead between your thumb and finger, as shown at left. Then tear off the end of the envelope that holds the bead, as shown.

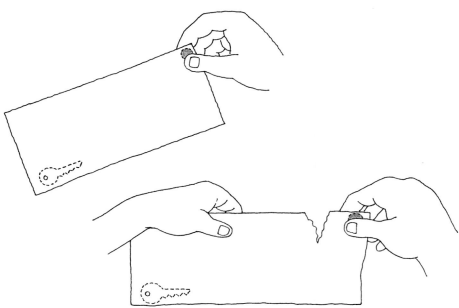

Keep the corner of the envelope and the bead between your fingers and hand the rest of the envelope to a spectator. He removes the key and finds that it opens the lock!

While the interest of the audience is on this action, casually drop the torn corner of the envelope with the bead into your coat pocket, and all evidence of your trickery is gone. To your audience, it seems that you have proved your point about the psychic phenomenon of psychometry.

Author's note: I learned this trick from U. F. Grant and have used it to mystify audiences all over the world. This ingenious method was devised by the well-known magician Martin Sunshine.

A MEETING
OF MINDS

This mind magic trick is a demonstration of mind reading in reverse. You appear to make the spectators pick up your thoughts. You will need to cut five discs from stiff paper and to write the following letters on these discs exactly as shown below.

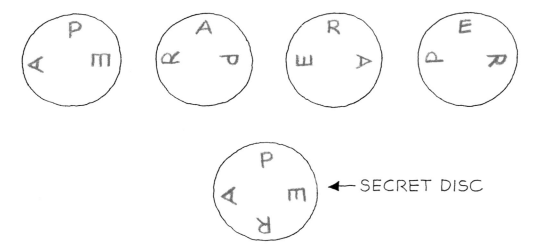

← SECRET DISC

Each of the four discs has a three-letter word on it: APE, RAP, ERA, or PER. The audience sees these. The fifth disc has four letters and is your secret disc, your "gimmick."

You will need to wear a hat for this performance so that you can hide this disc inside its inner band. You are now ready to go.

HERE'S WHAT YOU APPEAR TO DO

Show the spectators the four discs with the three-letter words on them. Place these discs faceup in a row in front of your audience and ask someone to be the receiver of your thoughts. Tell this person to make his mind as blank as possible while you try to project one of those four words into his mind. Talk to your spectators about thought projection using the following patter:

In this experiment with mind magic, you are going to be the telepathic recipient, and I will be the thought projector. Think of our communication as a kind of radio broadcasting in which a receiver set picks up the signal sent out by the transmitter.

For this test in thought transmission we will use these simple three-letter words APE, PER, ERA, *and* RAP. *To be a good telepathic receiver, make your mind blank and be receptive to what comes in.*

All right, let's try the experiment together. Now look these four words over and mentally decide which word comes most powerfully to your mind.

I will now gather the discs and drop them into a hat. Remember the word that had the most powerful effect on your mind while I am selecting the disc with the word that came most powerfully to my mind.

Reach into the hat and remove one of the discs.

Here it is. Before I show you which one it is, name out loud the word that came most strongly to your mind.

The spectator names the word.

Terrific! You have been a splendid telepathic receiver! You have succeeded in picking up the word I projected to your mind.

You reach the grand finale of the trick when you show the word on the disc you hold—the very word the person named!

HERE'S HOW IT WORKS

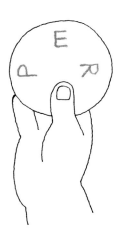

As you already know, five discs are actually used in this trick. Four of those discs have three-letter words on them, while the fifth disc (the one you hid in the inner band of your hat) has four letters on it. When you reach into the hat to take out a disc, remove this "gimmick" disc upside down so that no one can see what word is on it.

Ask the spectator to name the word he "received" most powerfully. Because your secret disc has all four letters used in each of the three-letter discs, all you have to do is to shift the disc in your hands until the desired word is visible. Cover the extra letter with your thumb when you show the disc, as indicated in the drawing below. Your audience will never suspect this simple deception.

THE ANSWER
TO YOUR QUESTION

This is a mind-reading act in which you appear to mysteriously know the questions that your spectators have asked before they ask them out loud. You appear to give these answers without knowing yourself what the questions are. You seem to be under a sort of magical, clairvoyant spell.

All you need to create this effect are your hat and enough slips of paper and pencils so that several spectators can join in the fun.

You will also need to use a certain amount of finesse.

Distribute slips of paper to various people in your audience. Tell each person who receives a slip to write down a question that he or she would like to have answered. After your spectators have written their questions, tell them to crumple up the slips. Pass around the hat to collect the slips, and after several questions have been dropped into it, reach into the hat and stir them up.

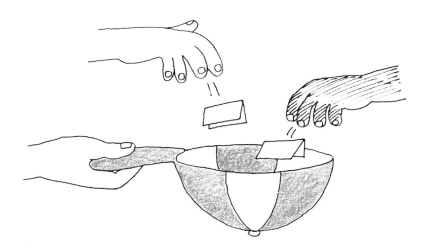

After all the slips have been collected, bring the hat back to the stage (or the part of the room that serves as your stage).

One by one, remove the slips from the hat, and without opening them, hold them to your forehead and answer the questions for the spectators. You seem to be a medium, or clairvoyant, who knows things without knowing how you know them.

HERE'S HOW
IT WORKS

While collecting the slips in the hat, reach your hand in to stir them up and casually pick up one of the slips. Open that slip as you pass through the audience gathering the slips, and glance down briefly to read it in such a way that you conceal your purpose.

Memorize the question on the slip that you have opened, fold it up again, and slip it under the inner band of the hat. With the hat on the table in front of you, tell the spectators that you will now try to read their minds. Try to answer each question for them without looking at the question.

Reach into the hat and take out a crumpled slip, and without opening it, hold it to your forehead. Answer the first question, the one you have just read in secret.

After answering this question, open the slip you are holding under the pre-

text of checking the question to see if you answered it correctly. As you read it, memorize the question on this slip while calling out the question that you have just answered. Have the person in the audience whose question you have answered tell you whether or not you are right. Then place the slip aside.

Reach into the hat again and take out another question and hold the crumpled slip to your forehead. Answer this slip by answering the second question, which you have just memorized. After answering, open the slip and memorize the question just as you did before. Pretend that you are reading the second question out loud as you are memorizing the third. You will then be ready to answer the third question from what is apparently the third slip, as you removed it from the hat.

Continue answering all of the questions in the hat, keeping one question ahead each time. Finally, when you have gone through all of the questions in the hat, take the last slip out (the one you have concealed under the inner band) and pretend to answer it, while you are really answering the last question you memorized.

You will amaze your audience by answering all of their questions. Remember, though, you are an entertainer, not a psychiatrist, so keep your answers lighthearted. Some people take the words of a medium very seriously.

DEAD OR ALIVE?

The world of the spirits is closely tied to mind magic. Here is a trick that will lead your audience to think you are in touch with the spirits of people who have died. All you need is your hat, pencils, and a sheet of paper.

HERE'S WHAT YOU APPEAR TO DO

Tear a sheet of paper into eight pieces. Hand these to the spectators with the request that four of them write down the initials of people who they know are alive and the other four write down the initials of people from the past. You can direct them to think about well-known people who lived a long time ago, such as George Washington and Harriet Tubman. When they have done this, they fold the slips and drop them into the hat. Shake the hat to mix up the slips. Reach into the hat and take out one of the slips. Without looking at it, you instantly declare whether the slip has the initials of a living person or those of a person who has died. When the slip is opened, you are found to be correct. Repeat this for the remaining seven slips, knowing without fail which slips name a person from the living and which a person from the dead.

HERE'S HOW IT WORKS　To perform this trick, tear the original sheet of paper in the manner shown in this drawing:

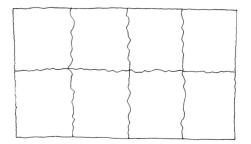

Notice that when you tear the paper in this way, four of the pieces of paper will have two smooth edges, while the other four will have only one.

When you hand out these pieces of paper to the spectators, give the slips with two smooth edges to those people who are to write the initials of a living person. Give the slips with only one smooth edge to those people who are to write the initials of a person from the past.

The slips are then folded and collected in the hat. As you reach into the hat and remove each slip in turn, it is a simple matter to feel the edges so that you know whether to announce that it has the initials of a living person or one who has died.

You will find that people will make far more of this trick than you might expect. You seem to be a medium with a special connection to the world of the spirits. You may even spook your audience with your clairvoyant mind-reading power!

MODUS OPERANDI:
ESP

The last two tricks in this book are especially challenging. In this one, you demonstrate your ability to use extrasensory perception—ESP—to guess the name your spectator is thinking of. The modus operandi (how it works) will be described at the same time as the effect of your trick on the spectator.

You will need only two slips of paper, each about 2 by 3 inches (5 by 8 centimeters). Give the spectator one of the slips and tell her to fold it three times. Start to fold your own slip to show her how she should do this.

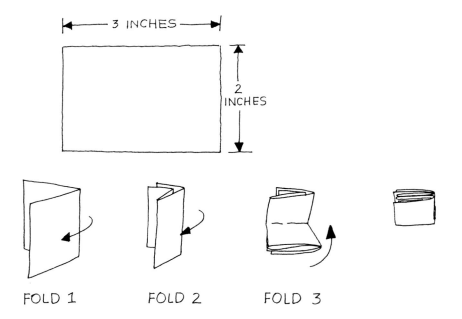

<- 3 INCHES ->

2 INCHES

FOLD 1   FOLD 2   FOLD 3

Then ask the spectator to unfold her slip, turn her back, and write on the slip any name that comes to mind. Tell her to refold her slip with the name inside.

Having done this, she turns to face you again. Tell her that you will keep your slip in your pocket until it is needed later in the experiment.

Pretend to place your slip in your left hand, but really palm it into your right hand. (Practice this move to make sure you conceal the slip successfully.) Place your closed left hand in your left coat pocket and pull it out again empty. The

action is so casual that, as far as your audience is concerned, you have simply placed your blank slip aside in your pocket.

Now comes the clever move. With the slip palmed in your right fingers, reach over to inside your left sleeve at the elbow and pull it up a bit. As you do this, tuck the slip that is palmed in your right fingers into a fold of cloth at the elbow bend of the sleeve.

Then, holding your left arm slightly bent so as to keep the slip tucked in there, reach over with your left hand and pull up your right sleeve in the same manner. These perfectly natural gestures will leave you with empty hands.

Now ask another spectator to come forward and act as a witness to the ESP experiment that is now under way.

Have the volunteer stand on your right and the first spectator on your left. As you gesture to where the volunteer is to stand, your right sleeve will drop down a bit. Using your left hand, you pull it up again, and you follow through by pulling up your left sleeve with your right hand once more.

This gives you the chance to palm the slip into your right hand. All of this is a tricky way to convince any doubtful spectators that you have indeed put the slip of paper in your left pocket. You have pulled up your sleeves and showed them your empty hands!

Now that you have palmed the slip once more in your right hand, you are ready to proceed. Take the spectator's folded slip with your left hand. Pretend to place it in your right fingers, but really keep it in your left hand by closing your fingers over it, revealing instead the slip that you concealed in your right hand. This is called a perfect billet switch.

Without any interruption of movement, the blank slip is handed to the second spectator to hold. As soon as this is done, say that you will use the blank slip you placed in your pocket to complete the test.

Reach into your left coat pocket and bring out the slip you palmed in your left hand. This is really the slip that had the name written on it, but to the spectator it seems that you merely removed the blank slip you placed there a few moments before.

Open the slip and pretend to write something on it with a pencil. This gives you a chance to secretly read the name written by the first spectator. Refold this slip and hand it to the second spectator while you take back the slip that spectator had been holding.

Now open this slip (which is really blank, but which the second spectator thinks has the name that the first spectator wrote). Call out the name (actually the name you have just learned from the other slip).

Then ask the second spectator to open the slip he is holding and read the name written on it. He does so, and the names match!

This is an advanced trick that demands subtle movements. By practicing it, you will learn some good lessons about performing mind magic: Avoid all fast movements; perform in a natural and casual manner; remember that mind magic is designed to fool the minds of the spectators, not their eyes.

THE MASTERMIND

This trick produces one of my favorite effects. The previous trick convinced your spectators that you had the gift of ESP. Now you will really confuse them. Your spectators will be astonished to find that they possess this mystifying gift as well. To begin, you will need a stack of twenty-five blank business cards (or you can make them yourself out of stiff paper).

HERE'S WHAT YOU APPEAR TO DO

Count off nine cards and hand them to a volunteer to examine. Line them up in a row on a table.

Write a number on each from one to nine. As you write each number on a card, turn that card facedown. When you write number nine, place it to one side and ask your volunteer to remember that number on that particular card.

A spectator then picks up the rest of the cards, mixes them up, and places them number-side down to the table. Obviously no one has the slightest idea which number is where in the row of cards.

At this point, ask the spectator to try his hand at ESP. Ask him to point to the card that he thinks is number one. Pick up the card that he points to and place it on the stack you are holding. Write a number one on its back.

Then ask the spectator to use his ESP again and point to the card that he thinks is number two. Go through this process until there are only two cards left on the table: number eight, apparently, and the number nine that was placed to the side. Pick up "what may be the number eight card" and place it blank-side up on the stack. Glance at the spectator and ask him to recall which number was on the card placed to one side. Naturally he says, "It is number nine." The back of this card is so numbered, as is the number eight. Place the number eight card on your stack and the number nine card on top of it.

All is now ready for the amazing climax of the trick. Immediately deal out the cards on the table from number nine through number one. Ask the spectator to turn over each card to see how he did with his ESP. The suspense mounts as each card is turned over. He is correct every time!

Prepare the blank cards for this effect ahead of time. Write a number one on both sides of the first card, a number two on both sides of the second card, and so on up through number seven. Stack them in order with the number seven card on top.

Place these pre-numbered cards on top of the stack of blank cards. Then, on one side only of another card, write a number eight and place it blank-side up on top of the stack.

Now turn the entire stack over so that these prepared cards are all on the bottom and the unprepared blank cards are on the top. Put a small pencil dot on top of the blank card, so that you can tell at a glance when this side of the stack is on top. Wrap the stack with a rubber band and put it in your coat pocket along with a marking pen. You are now ready to begin.

Ask any spectator who would like to test his or her powers of ESP to come forward. Bring out the stack of blank cards and the marking pen from your pocket. Remove the rubber band and hold the stack so that the pre-numbered cards are on the bottom (resting against your palm) and the unprepared cards

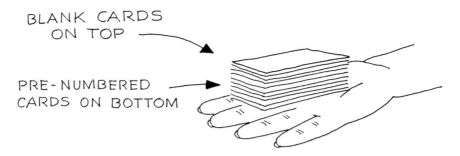

are on top (a glance at the pencil dot assures you of this).

Deal off nine blank cards and hand them to a spectator, who places them in a row on the table. Place the rest of the stack of cards aside for the moment.

Take the marking pen and number the cards, one at a time, from one through nine. Pick up the number nine card and place it to one side, while you say, "I will turn this number nine card back down on the table and place it to one side as a special card for you to concentrate on. Remember that it is number nine."

Ask the spectator to pick up the other cards, to turn them all numbered-side down, to mix them thoroughly, and to put them back in a row on the table blank-side up. No one knows where any of the numbers are now, except for the number nine.

Now suggest that the ESP test begin. Ask the spectator to run his hand slowly along above the row of cards. Tell him that when he gets a hunch, he should touch the card he thinks is number one. The spectator does this.

Pick this card up without showing the number on its other side and place it directly on top of the stack of blank cards that you have meanwhile picked up and are holding in your left hand. Take the marking pen and write a number one on it.

Ask the spectator to get a hunch as to which card he thinks is number two. Pick up the card that he points to, place it on the stack in your left hand in the same way as before, and write a number two on it. Keep going in this way through all of the numbered cards up through number seven. This leaves two cards on the table.

Pick up "what may be the number eight card" and place it on the stack. Now comes the subtle move that brings about the magical effect. At this point, suddenly ask the spectator if he can remember the number of the remaining card that you placed to the side. He naturally says, "It is number nine." You take the marking pen and number it nine right on the table.

This gives you the perfect chance to drop your left hand to your side and secretly turn over the stack of cards. The pre-numbered cards are now on top, and the others are on the bottom, as simple as that.

Since the bottom card is the blank side of the number eight card, the stack looks exactly the same as before as far as the spectators are concerned. (Marking number nine on the back of the card on the table allows you the perfect chance to make this secret move.) Having marked a number nine on the card on the table, move it toward the stack in your left hand.

Take note of the blank card on the top of the stack, as you say, "And this one, of course, we will mark as number eight." Mark it accordingly, then place the number nine card on top of it.

Now simply deal out the cards in a row on the table from number nine through number one. One by one, you turn each card over and show that the number matches exactly on each side. The volunteer appears to have been 100 percent right in his attempt at ESP.

This is a very clever feat of mind magic. When performed smoothly, it is entirely mystifying and will leave a lasting impression on the spectators. It is especially fascinating to the spectators because it is one of them and not the performer who seems to be the wizard. Naturally, though, everyone really knows that you are the real mastermind behind the scenes.

MORE ABOUT MAGIC

Bailey, Vanessa. *Magic Tricks: Games and Projects for Children.* New York: Franklin Watts, 1990.

Beisner, Monika. *Secret Spells and Curious Charms.* New York: Farrar, Straus, & Giroux, 1986.

Bird, Malcolm, and Alan Dart. *The Magic Handbook.* San Francisco: Chronicle Books, 1992.

Border, Rosy. *Beginner's Guide to Magic.* Aspen, Colo.: Mad Hatter Publications, 1992.

Collis, Len. *Magic Tricks for Children.* Hauppauge, N.Y.: Barron, 1989.

Day, Jon. *Let's Make Magic: Over Forty Tricks You Can Do.* New York: Kingfisher Books, 1992.

Friedhoffer, Bob. *The Magic Show: A Guide for Young Magicians.* Brookfield, Conn.: The Millbrook Press, 1994.

Lewis, Shari, and Dick Zimmerman. *Shari Lewis Presents One Hundred-One Magic Tricks for Kids to Do.* New York: Random House Books for Young Readers, 1990.

McGill, Ormond. *Paper Magic: Creating Fantasies and Performing Tricks With Paper.* Brookfield, Conn.: The Millbrook Press, 1992.

Watermill Press Staff. *Kid's Book of Magic Tricks.* Mahway, N.J.: Troll Associates, 1992.

Wyler, Rose, and Gerald Ames. *Magic Secrets.* New York: HarperCollins, 1991.

INDEX

ABOUT THE AUTHOR

Ormond McGill is a world-acclaimed magician who has been practicing his art for half a century. He has toured internationally with his stage shows East Indian Miracles and South Sea Island Magic.

His numerous books on magic include, for adults, *Entertaining with Magic, Atomic Magic, Psychic Magic,* and the *Encyclopedia of Stage Illusions,* and, for young readers, *Balancing Magic and Other Tricks, Science Magic: 101 Tricks You Can Do, Paper Magic,* and *Voice Magic.*

A resident of northern California, Ormond tours, gives lectures, and does magic shows for children and adults.